Meeting Funder Compliance

A Case Study of Challenges, Time Spent, and Dollars Invested

Sandraluz Lara-Cinisomo, Paul Steinberg

Supported by the Forbes Funds, a supporting organization of the Pittsburgh Foundation

LABOR AND POPULATION

The research described in this report was supported by the Forbes Funds, a supporting organization of the Pittsburgh Foundation, and through the RAND Corporation's continuing program of self-initiated independent research. This research was conducted within RAND Labor and Population, a unit of the RAND Corporation.

Library of Congress Cataloging-in-Publication Data

Lara-Cinisomo, Sandraluz.
    Meeting funder compliance : a case study of challenges, time spent, and dollars invested / Sandraluz Lara-Cinisomo, Paul Steinberg.
      p. cm.
    "MG-505."
    Includes bibliographical references.
    ISBN 0-8330-3956-3 (pbk.)
      1. Nonprofit organizations—Management—Case studies. 2. Nonprofit organizations—Finance—Case studies. I. Steinberg, Paul, 1953– II. Rand Corporation. III. Title.

HD62.6.L37 2006
658'.048—dc22

                                                                                        2006012909

The RAND Corporation is a nonprofit research organization providing objective analysis and effective solutions that address the challenges facing the public and private sectors around the world. RAND's publications do not necessarily reflect the opinions of its research clients and sponsors.

RAND® is a registered trademark.

Published 2006 by the RAND Corporation
1776 Main Street, P.O. Box 2138, Santa Monica, CA 90407-2138
1200 South Hayes Street, Arlington, VA 22202-5050
4570 Fifth Avenue, Suite 600, Pittsburgh, PA 15213-2612
RAND URL: http://www.rand.org/
To order RAND documents or to obtain additional information, contact
Distribution Services: Telephone: (310) 451-7002;
Fax: (310) 451-6915; Email: order@rand.org

Preface

The Forbes Funds, a supporting organization of the Pittsburgh Foundation, sponsors applied research designed to generate practical information on strategic issues to help Pittsburgh nonprofits to better serve the community. These efforts are supported through the Tropman Fund for Nonprofit Research. The mission of the Tropman Fund is to support applied research on strategic issues that are likely to have profound effects on nonprofit management and governance, especially among human service and community development organizations. Previous studies have explored capacity-building barriers and recommendations, performance in nonprofit organizations, and other relevant topics. These studies have helped inform the larger nonprofit community and have encouraged exemplary practices.

To add to this body of literature, the Forbes Funds commissioned the RAND Corporation to conduct a case study of the challenges, time investments, and costs from salaries associated with meeting funder compliance.

The research described in this report was supported by the Forbes Funds, a supporting organization of the Pittsburgh Foundation, and through the RAND Corporation's continuing program of self-initiated independent research. Support for such research is provided, in part, by donors and by the independent research and development provisions of RAND's contracts for the operation of its U.S. Department of Defense federally funded research and development centers. This research was conducted within RAND Labor and Population, a unit of the RAND Corporation.

Contents

Figures

Tables

Summary

Introduction

Funders provide financial support to nonprofit organizations, which, in turn, use the funding to implement programs that provide services to clients. A key part of this relationship is the need for nonprofits to ensure funding compliance—that is, the need to report program progress and expenditures to funders. While meeting funding compliance is clearly an issue, we do not clearly understand the management process within the nonprofit sector, especially how it relates to staff time investments in tracking outcomes and reporting results. To date, there is no systematic study that examines investments nonprofit staff make to meet funder compliance.

According to Charity Navigator, which charts the performance of nonprofits, there are 193 charitable organizations in Pennsylvania (Charity Navigator, undated). The Forbes Funds has taken the initiative, by creating the Tropman Fund for Nonprofit Research, to develop and fund research projects that will inform the larger nonprofit community. Previous studies have explored capacity-building barriers and recommendations, performance in nonprofit organizations, and other relevant topics, and have helped inform the larger nonprofit community. To add to this body of literature, the Forbes Funds commissioned the RAND Corporation to conduct a case study of the challenges, time spent, and costs associated with meeting funder compliance.

By nature, a case study enables researchers to explore areas in which little or no empirical data exist. This study exploits the inherent attributes of a case study to explore the experiences of staff meeting funder compliance, challenges in meeting funder compliance, and staff time investments in such activities, and solicits staff recommendations at the agency and funder level. Inherent in the case study methodology is the size of the sample. Thus, case studies tend to have fewer observations than other methodologies. In this study, we focus on one large site to examine in depth the challenges in meeting funder compliance, as well as time and dollars invested in meeting compliance. This study is guided by five research questions developed in partnership with the Forbes Funds:

1. How are staffing decisions made as they relate to compliance tasks?
2. What are the staffing challenges in meeting funder compliance?
3. What are the data challenges in meeting compliance?
4. What is the subjective experience of staff in meeting compliance?
5. What are the overall costs, in time and dollars, of meeting compliance?

The results reported are based on qualitative and quantitative data. Management and field staff from a local nonprofit were interviewed: management staff (seven directors and seven supervisors) were interviewed individually, and field staff (27 staff members providing direct services to families either off or on site) were interviewed in five focus groups during normally scheduled meeting times.

Key Findings

What we found is that staffing decisions are predetermined by a person's job description. Staffing challenges ranged from poor staff performance to overwhelmed staff. A closer examination of staff training showed that staff members report that they are not receiving adequate training for certain required tasks, which might explain why management staff reported field staff shortcomings as a staffing challenge.

General challenges reported included all parties involved—funders, the agency, and internal staff—suggesting that no one entity or group is primarily responsible for challenges experienced by staff. However, these challenges varied among staff. Management staff felt that the lack of internal agency protocol is a key factor, while field staff saw funders as the primary barrier and put equal burden on the agency and internal staff.

Numerous data challenges were cited by staff interviewed for this study, including limited access to necessary data, inadequate internal data, poor data computation methods, tedious data requested by funders, and unreliable internal staff. The primary data challenge for management staff was access to the data, while field staff said that the quality of the data was their primary challenge.

With regard to the organization's last compliance activity, five types of experiences were expressed, with the majority of directors and field staff reporting that the experience was stressful because of the type of data funders requested or because of the short turnaround time allowed to provide the necessary data. Supervisors said they experienced stress resulting from a lack of internal agency protocol and from the routine nature of their last experience. Our study found that 11 percent of the organization's funds were spent on compliance activities. While 11 percent may be difficult to situate because of a lack of comparison data, this study is one of the most accurate accounts of one organization's compliance-related expenditures, making future comparisons possible.

Recommendations

Based on staff response to questions about challenges to meeting funder compliance, it is clear that internal measures are needed to decrease the strain on staff and increase staff performance with regard to compliance activities. While the study site has plans to launch an agency-wide data system, there are vital infrastructure and personnel matters that must be addressed in conjunction with the data system. We recommend that other nonprofits in the region use the data collected to examine challenges their respective staff face in meeting funder compliance and provide solutions to those barriers.

With regard to funders, we recommend that they evaluate their data collection methods and type of requests to ensure the collection of pertinent data that will inform all participants (i.e., agency, funder, client, and staff), consider the burden placed on staff, consider how the data requested are being used, and consider having discussions with clients related to compliance that are sensitive to the power differential between agency and funder.

Next Steps

As a result of this study, survey items were developed that can be piloted with a random selection of organizations and revised for implementation with a larger sample of nonprofits. The instruments in the appendixes will serve as a guide for further investigation. Additional items about the cost of materials and facilities (e.g., rent, utilities, etc.) will be required for a more detailed analysis of the cost of meeting funder compliance. Finally, this case study exploits the experience of only one side of the process, the nonprofit side, which calls for an exploration of the compliance process from the funder side.

Acknowledgments

The authors gratefully acknowledge funding for this report from the Forbes Funds. We especially appreciate the support, collaboration, and patience of the executive director of Providing for Families for opening his doors and books for this study. In addition, we would like to thank the staff of Providing for Families for their candid responses and time. This study could not have been possible without their participation. We are also grateful for support from donors and through the independent research and development provisions of RAND's contracts and development centers.

CHAPTER ONE

Introduction

Background

Working together, funders provide financial support to nonprofit organizations, which, in turn, use the funding to implement programs that
provide services to clients. A key part of this relationship is the need for
nonprofits to ensure funding compliance—that is, the need to report
program progress and expenditures to funders. On the funder side,
funders have specific regulations that nonprofits must follow in reporting fiscal investments and completing outcome measures, and funders
must deal with multiple nonprofits, each of which has its own method
for tracking and reporting inputs and outputs. On the nonprofit side,
nonprofit organizations must follow the funding compliance guidance
from a funder, and nonprofits often must deal with multiple funders,
each of which has its own specific reporting requirements and dead-
lines. These compliance-reporting requirements are on top of other
reporting activities that nonprofits must engage in. Thus, nonprofits
face competing time investments, especially when these organizations
are managed in a way that increases the level of involvement by staff in
such activities.

  While meeting funding compliance is clearly an important issue,
we do not completely understand the management process within the
nonprofit sector (Gawande and Wheeler, 1999), especially as it relates
to staff time investments in tracking and reporting time investments
and dollars spent on specific administrative tasks. To date, there is no
systematic study that examines investments made by nonprofit staff to
meet funder compliance. While the accuracy of personnel time track-

ing has been explored, investments made in time and dollars were not examined (Wing and Hager, 2004). Wing and Hager (2004) showed that tracking personnel time was a low priority among the nine non-profits studied. While this study did not explore the challenges and costs associated with meeting funder compliance, and while there has not been an examination of the amount funders allow for compliance activities, there is a growing interest among scholars in nonprofits' administrative and fiscal practices.

In the last two decades, there has been a growing body of literature on management costs in nonprofits (see Hager and Greenlee, 2004, for a review). Hager and Greenlee (2004) describe the recent history of nonprofit financial research and efforts made to measure nonprofits' financial performance. They note that among the pitfalls of this type of measurement are accounting problems on the part of nonprofits and rampant noncompliance. Others have also noted similar difficulties in measuring nonprofits' fiscal activities (Wing and Hager, 2004). Hager and Greenlee (2004) also point out that a lack of nonprofit financial data makes comparing nonprofits with private businesses difficult. Still, recent efforts have been aimed at understanding the financial practices of nonprofits (see, for example, Gammal et al., 2005; Pollak, Rooney, and Hager, 2001). For example, one specific area of interest has been nonprofits' experience in working with funders.

Recently, the Stanford Project on the Evolution of Nonprofits (SPEN) at Stanford University completed a two-year investigation of nonprofits in the Bay Area and found that many funders differ in their criteria for acheiving compliance, which created conflicts for nonprofits (Gammal et al., 2005). While this study is the first to examine the general experiences of management staff within nonprofits in working with funders, it does not investigate systematically nonprofits' challenges and experiences in meeting funder compliance, nor do any other studies. Additionally, there is no literature that describes the types of activities in which nonprofit staff engage in meeting funder compliance. Moreover, there are no data on the amount of time nonprofit staff spend on compliance-related activities. Finally, there are no empirical data that can quantify how much, in dollars, is invested in meeting funder compliance. Gunz, Macnaughton, and Wensley (1995) provide some insight into the costs associated with meeting funder compliance in their study of 51 Canadian companies. This study found that after taking into account the size of the company, 1 to 3.4 percent of grant funds were spent on funder compliance. However, the authors caution against drawing conclusions based on these results because some companies included the costs of getting the grant while others did not. Other studies have found that difficulties in estimating such investments are due to vague guidelines for reporting, a lack of tracking, and poor reporting practices on the part of nonprofits (Pollack and Rooney, 2003).

According to Charity Navigator, which charts the performance of nonprofits, there are 193 charitable organizations in Pennsylvania (Charity Navigator, undated). The Forbes Funds has taken the initiative, by creating the Tropman Fund for Nonprofit Research, to develop and fund research projects that will inform the larger nonprofit community. Previous studies have explored capacity-building barriers and recommendations, performance in nonprofit organizations, and other relevant topics and have helped inform the larger nonprofit community.

Objectives

With funding from the Tropman Fund for Nonprofit Research at the Forbes Funds, RAND sought to add to this body of literature, in particular by looking at the nonprofit side of the relationship with funders and assessing the challenges and costs nonprofits face in meeting funder compliance.[1] Specifically, this study reports on the results of a case study of a local nonprofit organization[2] to determine how the organization makes staffing decisions and carries out compliance-related activities, how much time it invests in these tasks, and how this time translates

---

[1] This case study does not exploit the processes, challenges, and decisions surrounding compliance on the funder side.

[2] The case study organization was chosen from nonprofits within Western Pennsylvania, based on the location of the Forbes Funds in Pittsburgh, Pennsylvania; work on this project was conducted in the RAND Corporation's Pittsburgh office.

into dollars spent. As described in the above, there are no empirical data that tell us about the types of activities in which nonprofit staff engage to meet funder compliance. While there are some qualitative data on how executives in nonprofits experience funder compliance activities, there is no systematic analysis of those experiences among all nonprofit staff who engage in those activities. Additionally, there are no data on the amount of time staff devote to compliance-related activities. While there are some data on the financial investments non-profits make in meeting funder compliance, there are serious concerns regarding the accuracy of those numbers. Therefore, a case study was carried out to identify the types of tasks staff from a selected nonprofit engage in to meet funder compliance and to examine staff experiences in meeting funder compliance. This case study also includes an analysis of the amount of time and money spent on such activities.

By nature, a case study enables researchers to explore areas in which little or no empirical data exist. This study exploits the inherent attributes of a case study to explore the experiences of staff in meeting funder compliance, challenges in meeting funder compliance, and staff time investment in such activities, and solicits staff recommendations at the agency and funder level. Inherent in the case study methodology is the size of the sample. Thus, case studies tend to have fewer observations than other methodologies. In this study, we focus on one large site to examine in depth the challenges in meeting funder compliance, as well as time and dollars invested in meeting compliance.

This study is guided by five research questions developed in partnership with the Forbes Funds that aim to address the gaps in the literature, as noted above, regarding funder compliance. The five research questions are:

1. How are staffing decisions made as they relate to funder compliance tasks?
2. What are the staffing challenges in meeting funder compliance?
3. What are the data challenges in meeting funder compliance?
4. What is the subjective experience of staff in meeting funder compliance?

5. What are the overall costs, in time and dollars, of meeting funder compliance?

Approach

To answer the five questions, the study included the results of open-ended and closed-ended questions administered to management staff (directors and supervisors) and field staff (staff providing direct services to families either off or on site) of the chosen case study site—Providing for Families (PFF).[3] Below, we discuss the site, the sample, the procedures used, the interview instruments, and the data analysis conducted.

Site

PFF is a nonprofit organization located in Western Pennsylvania that focuses on preventing and treating child abuse. PFF was selected as the case study site by the Forbes Funds' executive director because of its staff size, annual revenue, complexity of funding streams, and the willingness of its executive director to open his books and involve his staff. Like many nonprofits, PFF receives funding from a variety of agencies, including the county and the state, as well as private foundations and the United Way. Each of these funding sources provides for a range of services. In some instances, one funding source may provide for numerous programs, while other funders may limit their support to specific activities. Staff interviewed for this study all engage in compliance and may be paid through numerous funding sources. Therefore, results for this study are for combined funding for fiscal year 2004–2005 rather than for a specific funder type or source.

---

[3] To protect the privacy of the case study site, the description of the agency is designed to provide relevant background information without revealing the actual study site. Thus, the name used throughout—Providing for Families—is a pseudonym.

Sample

For this study, three types of employees were interviewed: directors and supervisors (also referred to as management staff) and field staff. These individuals were selected for this study because they are directly involved in funder compliance activities.[4] Individual interviews were conducted with directors and supervisors, while focus group interviews were conducted with field staff. Focus groups were established by type of program to eliminate conflict in compliance engagement within focus groups. Focus groups met during regularly scheduled meetings without the presence of a supervisor. A total of 41 staff members were interviewed: seven directors, seven supervisors, and 27 field staff.

Procedures

To answer the five research questions, the study collected qualitative and quantitative data. RAND research staff administered a structured interview to directors and supervisors, consisting of open- and closed-ended questions; each interview took approximately 60 minutes. Each focus group consisted of three to seven participants. Focus groups were used for field staff because they potentially elicit participants' insights about complex issues (Keim et al., 1999), such as challenges in meeting funder compliance. Focus groups were also used because they allow researchers to collect data from a number of participants at one given time, thus reducing time and dollars required to conduct the study. Focus groups also included closed- and open-ended questions and took approximately 45 minutes. Focus group interviews were tape-recorded. In addition, with the exception of one respondent, each focus group participant completed a confidential demographics questionnaire. To protect the privacy of each participant, identification numbers were assigned.

Interview Instruments

Appendixes A, B, and C include copies of the interview instruments designed for this study. At the time of our study, no interview pro-

---

[4] Administrative assistants may provide support for such activities. However, for this study, administrative assistants were not interviewed.

tocol had been designed to collect information on time investments in compliance activities. Thus, following the general principles of cost measurement for early childhood programs delineated in Karoly et al. (2001) and the protocols developed for the 1995 Cost, Quality, and Child Outcomes Study (Helburn et al., 1995), we developed interview protocols for the study that allowed us to collect comprehensive cost data for each cost-specific compliance activity, including time investments. These data were used to estimate the overall organizational costs of meeting compliance. Costs included staff wages and did not include non-wage benefits; facilities costs (e.g., rent, utilities, etc.); or the value of equipment, materials, and supplies required to meet compliance. In most instances, the same questions were asked of directors, supervisors, and field staff. However, when appropriate, management and field staff were asked unique questions.

Data Analysis

Data analysis occurred in two stages: analysis of the qualitative data, followed by the analysis of the quantitative data.

Qualitative Analysis. The qualitative data were aggregated and summarized to provide an overall experience by staff type, and were used to answer questions 2, 3, and 4 (What are the staffing challenges in meeting funder compliance? What are the data challenges in meeting funder compliance? and What is the subjective experience of staff in meeting funder compliance?).

The purpose of the qualitative interview was to provide funders with a sense of the real-life experiences of nonprofit staff who are charged with meeting funder requirements and reporting results. Open-ended questions limit preconceived notions regarding staff experiences and allow participants to inform the analysis. This rich data should help funders understand the personal and personnel costs associated with meeting compliance, and should encourage funders to make adjustments to their requests that will help minimize any nonessential burden among nonprofit staff. In addition, the results should benefit the organization by identifying internal practices that may be creating barriers and undue burden while meeting funder compliance.

Using methods of grounded theory (Glazer and Strauss, 1967; Strauss and Corbin, 1990), an inductive process, we coded the responses. Next, responses to each open-ended question were grouped into meaningful categories. For instance, responses to the question about recent staff experience ranged from "stressful because a lot of people [are] involved" to "rewarding." Those derived categories were used to summarize the qualitative data. Where appropriate, quotes are used to illustrate a category or trend in participant responses.

Quantitative Analysis. The first research question was a closed-ended question that produced frequencies for each of the answer choices. As noted above, evaluations of nonprofits have not considered the costs of meeting compliance. Yet, cost information is essential for understanding the resources required to meet compliance and analyzing how cost-effective a nonprofit is. Thus, we analyzed the time and dollar investments necessary to meet funder compliance. Time spent was analyzed by computing the number of hours by task for all staff for an average month during fiscal year 2004–2005. To determine costs, we calculated dollars spent on salaries for each hour of staff training and time carrying out compliance-related tasks for one fiscal year. The cost data were used to answer research question 5 (What are the overall costs, in time and dollars, of meeting funder compliance?). Because of the type of data collected and the two-pronged approach to answering this question, the analysis related to this question is more rigorous.

Organization of This Report

The next chapter provides a brief overview of the case study site selected. Chapter Three reports findings based on the case study analysis and framed by the five research questions. Chapter Four presents conclusions and recommendations.

As noted above, Appendixes A, B, and C provide the interview protocols for the management staff interviews, the field staff focus groups, and field staff confidential interviews, respectively. Appendix D presents a distribution of compliance hours and compliance dollars.

CHAPTER TWO

Overview of Case Study Site

Before presenting the case study findings for the five research questions in Chapter Three, we provide a brief overview of the case study site.

Sources of PFF Revenue

As noted in Chapter One, PFF is a nonprofit organization whose revenue comes from the county and the state, as well as from private foundations and the United Way. Figure 2.1 shows the distribution of revenue from these four sources. Revenue from the county includes funds that are provided through government agencies, such as the Office of Children, Youth, and Families. State funds are derived solely from the Victims of Crime Act (VOCA) state program. Private funds include foundation dollars and restricted grants. Finally, United Way dollars comprise donations and allocations by United Way. The total revenue from these funding sources is $6,554,518.

Of that funding, the vast majority (89 percent) of the agency's revenue is composed of county funds, which pay for the majority of the programs offered by the organization. The smallest proportion of revenue comes from private funds, which total $418,636. Clearly, all funds also go toward paying for non-wage benefits, facilities (e.g., rent, utilities, etc.), and other operating costs. However, for this report, revenue from these sources was used only to determine the percentage of revenue used to pay for time invested in compliance activities. The cost of materials, such as paper, copy machines, and other office supplies, is not part of this study and therefore not included in this report.

**Figure 2.1
Distribution of Agency Revenue
Sources Included in This Study**

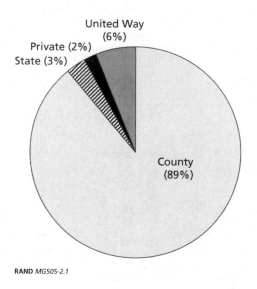

RAND *MG505-2.1*

Descriptive Statistics of the Case Study Sample

Table 2.1 provides summary statistics for the case study sample. An equal proportion of directors and supervisors were interviewed (17 percent), with 66 percent of the participants classified as field staff. The majority (63 percent) of the participants were white, non-Hispanic, followed by black, non-Hispanic (32 percent). A very small sample of Hispanics and those whose racial identities were listed as "Other" were also interviewed. The vast majority of the participants had a college degree or higher. Over half of the sample was female (78 percent). Participants' ages ranged from 24 to 57 years, with a mean of 37.61. Personnel salaries by type of employee show that mean annual income for directors was $69,000. On average, supervisors earned $43,476 per year. The mean annual income for field staff was $29,821. On average, staff reported working over 40 hours per week, with a mean of 46.26 hours per week. In summary, the average employee is white, non-Hispanic, female, highly educated, and works more than 40 hours per week. In addition to collecting demographic data on the staff, observations were made about the mood, tone, and overall climate of this nonprofit and its staff.

During the course of the data collection phase of the study, numerous visits were made to the various offices of the nonprofit. Each time a visit was made, the staff were punctual, prepared to participate in the interview, and were always very willing to answer the interview questions, whether in an individual interview or focus group discussion. In addition to being ideal interview participants, the entire staff was interested in providing information that would help inform our research. In addition, all of the offices were well-kept, staff treated us with professionalism, and we were made to feel welcome.

Table 2.1
Descriptive Statistics of Case Study Sample

Personnel Characteristics	Percent/Mean (standard deviation) (n = 41)
Employee type	
Director	17%
Supervisor	17%
Staff	66%
Race and ethnicity	
White, non-Hispanic	63%
Hispanic	2%
Black, non-Hispanic	32%
Other	2%
Education	
High school	7%
College degree	44%
Master's degree	44%
Doctoral degree	5%

Table 2.1—Continued

Personnel Characteristics	Percent/Mean (standard deviation) (n = 41)
Gender	
Male	22%
Female	78%
Age (years)	37.61 (9.45)
Annual salary[a] (dollars)	
Director	$69,000 ($16,104)
Supervisor	$43,476 ($4,272)
Staff	$29,821 ($2,815)
Weekly work hours[b]	
Scheduled	39.21 (2.82)
Actual	46.26 (10.25)

[a] Salaries were imputed using means for the appropriate employee type for two individuals who did not report annual income and for one unpaid intern. The intern was assigned a salary because he is taking the place of a paid staff member and requires agency resources.
[b] Employee-reported hours.

Funder Compliance Process

Since we are ultimately interested in funder compliance, we examined the order in which some of the funder compliance activities occurred, looking in particular at the process within one program of the nonprofit organization as it completed a funder compliance report. The process illustrated in Figure 2.2 is very comparable to other staff descriptions of the process for other programs. Based on the individual interviews and focus group discussions, we found that an average of six steps are needed to complete a funder compliance report and that the effort may involve up to four individuals.

As the figure shows, the first step occurs when the field staff member visits or meets with the client. She then writes a narrative of the visit and documents any necessary statistics or demographic data.

The field staff member provides a copy of the report to her direct supervisor and to an administrative assistant (AA). If the report has been handwritten, the AA may type it up. In cases where the report has been typed, the AA may proofread it. In addition, the AA puts a copy of the report in the appropriate file. The supervisor reviews the report and returns it to the field staff member with feedback. The field staff member then makes any necessary changes and returns it to her supervisor. Given that each field staff member has multiple cases, this process will be repeated numerous times. For the supervisor, this means multiple reports for each of her staff. When all of the reports have been finalized, the supervisor will summarize the information in a report to her director. The director then synthesizes the information from this report into a formal report to be provided to the funder.

Figure 2.2
Typical Process to Complete a Funder Compliance Report

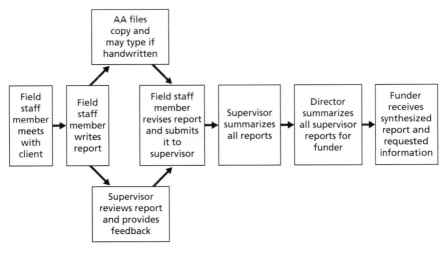

RAND *MG505-2.2*

Funder Compliance Activities Within the Funder Compliance Process

We were also interested in the specific types of funder compliance activities that were completed as part of the process and whether management staff and field staff participated in those tasks. Staff members were asked to describe the types of compliance activities they engaged in during the last fiscal year. The majority of those activities fell within one of the ten categories listed in Figure 2.3 for management staff (responses collected through interviews) and Table 2.2 for field staff (responses collected through focus groups). Without exception, there was no discrepancy within groups, primarily because focus groups were organized by program type, such as on-site therapists and in-home therapists, and included personnel with the same responsibilities.

Figure 2.3
Distribution of Management Engagement in Compliance Activities

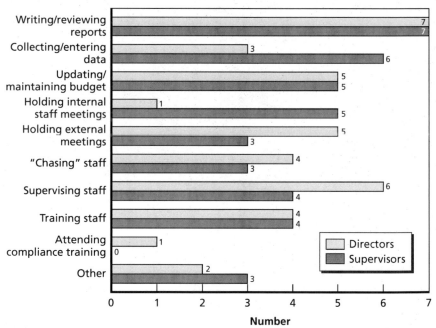

Figure 2.3 shows that all management staff are responsible for writing reports and reviewing staff reports. The majority of supervisors (six of seven) are responsible for collecting and entering data, such as the number of families serviced. An equal number of directors and supervisors (five of seven) are engaged in budgetary tasks, such as tracking program expenses. In contrast, five directors are responsible for attending external meetings related to compliance. Over half of the directors reported having to "chase" the staff they supervised, including supervisors, for data and reports necessary for funder compliance. Six directors and four supervisors, while responsible for supervising the staff, said they supervise tasks related to compliance activities. An equal number of management staff (four) said they train staff on funder compliance tasks, such as writing reports or collecting data. Only one director said she attends training sessions specifically about compliance regulations, and none of the supervisors reported engaging in this activity.[1] Two directors and three supervisors said they carry out other compliance activities, such as responding to funder requests and calling clients.

Table 2.2 shows the comparable results for field staff engaged in compliance activities during the last fiscal year. All field staff reported writing reports. The majority (three of five) of the groups said they collect and enter data to meet funder compliance and all update and maintain a budget. Three focus groups said they train other staff on compliance activities. Four focus groups said they attend internal staff meetings, but three groups said they do not attend external meetings. Fewer than half said they spend time chasing staff for information or supervising other staff.

---

[1] It was not clear whether supervisors were invited to such trainings or if all supervisors refused to attend.

Table 2.2
Distribution of Field Staff Engagement in Compliance Activities

Type of Compliance Task	Focus Groups Engaged in Task (n = 5 groups)		
	Yes	No	Missing
Writing reports	5	0	0
Collecting/entering data	3	1	1
Updating/maintaining budget	5	0	0
Attending internal staff meetings	4	1	0
Attending external meetings	—	3	2
"Chasing" staff	2	1	2
Supervising staff	2	1	2
Training staff	3	—	2
Attending compliance training	—	5	—

NOTE: The nature of focus group discussions allows participants to move the conversation from one topic to another. In cases where data are missing, the group discussion focused on other topics or questions, such as the staff workload.

CHAPTER THREE

Case Study Findings

In this chapter, we highlight the key findings, breaking them out according to the five research questions presented in Chapter One.

Research Question 1: How Are Staffing Decisions Made as They Relate to Funding Compliance Tasks?

With the exception of one director, all other management staff said they were responsible for delegating compliance tasks to staff. Of those who reported delegating tasks, all said they delegate based on staff job descriptions. Management staff reported that all service-delivery staff are required to document their visits and are required to produce reports that respond to funder requests regarding treatment, frequency of visits, and demographics. One director reported using additional criteria for delegating tasks, such as individual staff skills, staff ability, flexibility, and receptiveness to requests. Two supervisors said they also use prior staff experience and training levels as criteria.

Research Question 2: What Are the Staffing Challenges in Meeting Funder Compliance?

Directors and supervisors were asked an open-ended question about what staffing challenges they experience in meeting funder compliance. Based on management staff responses, we derived four categories of challenges, shown in Figure 3.1: lack of staff responsibility, staff workload, lack of qualified staff, and other challenges. *Lack of staff responsibility*, which refers to any staff member who neglects to meet timelines or disregards the importance of a task, was mentioned by an equal number of directors and supervisors. The second category, *staff workload*, refers to the pressures and numerous responsibilities staff members have that prevent them from either completing a compliance task or carrying it out as directed. Four directors and five supervisors said this was a staffing issue. More than half (four) of the directors reported a *lack of qualified staff* as a staffing challenge, referring to the lack of skills staff possess or to the absence of qualified staff. The final category, *other*, refers to "agency-funder mismatch" and "job difficulty." Three supervisors reported one of these staffing challenges. The responses in each category are not mutually exclusive.

Field Staff Training

In exploring staffing issues of management staff, field staff were asked about the training they received to prepare them to carry out the various compliance tasks they were responsible for in the past fiscal year. Table 3.1 shows the results from the focus group discussion on staff training. The results indicate that all staff members who participated in the focus group discussions said they were not trained by their direct supervisor to write reports, collect or enter data, or maintain or track a budget (e.g., expenses). Instead, three of the five groups said a peer in their respective teams trained them informally, while the remaining two said they experienced no formal or informal training.

Given the results, reported in Figure 2.3, indicating that four of seven supervisors reported training as a part of their compliance activities, there seems to be a discrepancy. This discrepancy may be explained by the way in which the question was interpreted by management staff, who were asked about time spent training staff—without mention of formal or informal training. The question posed to the focus groups asked about "formal training." However, all focus group participants said they were not trained formally by supervisors. They also said they did not receive any informal training. Instead, they learned by "shadowing" or "watching" their colleagues.

Figure 3.1
Staffing Challenges Reported by Management

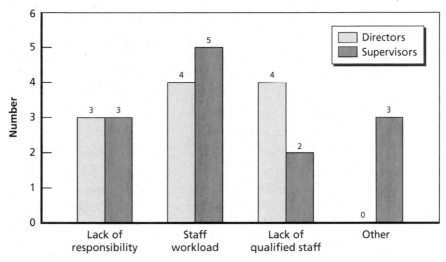

RAND *MG505-3.1*

Field staff said they did receive training associated with the direct services they provided, such as parent-teen interventions. However, according to field staff, supervisors did not provide training related to writing reports and other compliance activities. This discrepancy may also show that management staff perceive the training they provide to field staff as being sufficient to prepare them to carry out the various compliance tasks necessary, such as writing a report.

Table 3.1
Field Staff Training

Task	Number Receiving		
	Supervisor Training	Peer Training	No Training
Writing reports	0	3	2
Collecting/entering data	0	3	2
Updating/maintaining budgets	0	3	2

NOTE: n = 5.

General Challenges in Meeting Compliance

In addition to asking management staff about staffing challenges, all staff were asked about the challenges they face generally when completing a compliance activity, such as a report. Four general challenges emerged from the data: funder requirements, lack of an agency protocol, internal staff, and other. Table 3.2 shows the results from individual interviews with management staff and focus group interviews with field staff.

Funder requirements, which refers to the type and timing of requests, was reported by fewer than half of management staff but by four of five focus groups. During the focus group discussions, field staff highlighted their concerns about funder requests primarily because they are responsible for collecting the data required. In contrast, the majority of all staff reported that the *lack of an agency protocol*, which includes the fact that reports are not streamlined and that numerous staff are involved in one report, as a challenge. Management staff, in particular, seemed unhappy with the lack of clear and consistent procedures for meeting funder compliance. They reported that there were not clear steps toward meeting funder compliance other than completing a required report and submitting it to their respective superiors; field staff also expressed this frustration. *Internal staff* as a challenge refers to delays in responding to internal requests and lack of staff accountability. Three directors, one supervisor, and three focus groups cited this as a challenge to meeting funder compliance. Overall, the tone of staff accounts of *internal staff* as a challenge was one of frustration.

Table 3.2
Distributions of General Challenges Reported by Staff (Number)

Description	Directors (n = 7)	Supervisors (n = 7)	Focus Groups (n = 5 groups)
Funder requirements	3	3	4
Lack of agency protocol	5	5	3
Internal staff	3	1	3
Other	1	2	2

Many staff members seemed frustrated by the lack of responsiveness they experienced from their colleagues. This may also be related to a lack of agency protocol. One director, two supervisors, and two focus groups mentioned *other* challenges, such as lack of client participation and a heavy case management load.

Research Question 3: What Are the Data Challenges in Meeting Compliance?

Using an open-ended question, all participants were asked about data challenges they encounter when carrying out compliance activities, such as writing reports or providing data to funders. Based on the responses, six types of data challenges were derived: access to data (data access), quality of internal data (data quality), type of data requested by the funder (data required), data computation methods (data computation), internal staff, and other (see Figure 3.2).

Figure 3.2
Data Challenges Reported by Management

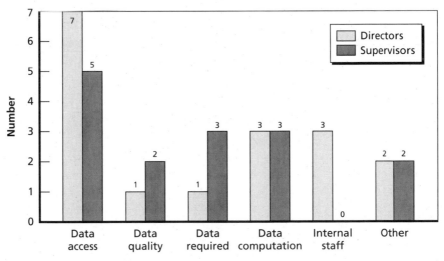

RAND *MG505-3.2*

Access to data refers to staff's inability to get to the necessary data because the data are not centralized or are not readily accessible because the data reside on an individual's hard drive. All seven directors and five supervisors said access to the data was a major challenge in carrying out compliance tasks. Management staff reported that everyone has their own database and is organized differently (e.g., some use software programs and others use notes), which made accessing the data difficult. *Quality of internal data* refers primarily to the lack of updated internal data provided by internal staff. Three supervisors reported type of data required by funders as a challenge; only one director reported this as a problem. In this instance, supervisors said that funders request data that require a significant investment of staff time and resources because the request may require numerous agency sources. An equal number (three) of directors and supervisors reported *data computation* methods as a data challenge. Management who reported this as a challenge said they often had to calculate numbers by hand because the data were not organized or stored in a way that allowed them to simply compute the required numbers. Directors are required to compile the data from their staff (supervisors and field staff). However, they tend to have less contact with field staff who collect much of the data and provide direct services. This may explain the next finding, which showed that three directors reported *internal staff* as a data challenge, while no supervisors reported this as a problem. *Other* data challenges include personal conflicts with client privacy. Close to a third of directors and supervisors reported this as a data challenge.

Focus group participants reported data challenges that fell within three categories: data quality, data type, and other. All focus groups reported *data quality* of internal data as a challenge, one focus group reported *data type* as a challenge, and one reported *other* data challenges.

Research Question 4: What Is the Subjective Experience of Staff in Meeting Compliance?

To explore the staff's subjective experience related to compliance activities, we asked them an open-ended question about their most recent experience in carrying out a compliance task. In the majority of the cases, staff used a report completed in the previous month as an example. As with previous research questions, responses were organized into meaningful categories using grounded theory, an inductive process. Five "experiences" were derived from the data: stressful because of funder request, stressful because of lack of agency protocol, routine, rewarding, and other. The responses are shown in Table 3.3.

Stressful because of funder request refers to strain staff felt from a funder's request due to the type of data or information requested or because of the time allowed to fill a request. The word "stressful" was used by the vast majority of participants and clearly reflects the tone used by staff when describing their most recent compliance activities. In this case, the majority of directors[1] (three) who answered this question and a majority of the focus groups (four) reported having experienced stress during the last compliance activity, but only one supervisor

Table 3.3
Distribution of Staff's Subjective Experience (Number)

Description	Directors (n = 5)	Supervisors (n = 6)	Focus Groups (n = 5 groups)
Stressful because of funder request	3	1	4
Stressful because of lack of agency protocol	2	4	1
Routine	1	4	1
Rewarding	0	1	2
Other	1	0	2

---

[1] Two directors did not provide a response to this question.

related such an experience.[2] *Stressful because of lack of agency protocol* refers to the stress staff felt because of the lack of clear steps or guidelines for carrying out a compliance task. A majority (four) of supervisors reported having this experience, while fewer directors and focus groups reported having had it. Again, the term "stressful" was used frequently. While the majority of supervisors reported feeling *stress because of a lack of agency protocol*, the same number reported their last experience as *routine* or part of their job. Two focus groups reported a *rewarding* experience (positive experience staff felt from reviewing the results of their work with families, as well as completing the report), having felt encouraged by seeing "family improvements." The same number of focus groups reported *other* experiences, such as reluctant clients. Again, the numbers are not mutually exclusive.

Research Question 5: What Are the Costs of Meeting Compliance?

The following are results from the cost analysis. Two dimensions of cost were investigated: time and dollars. Therefore, this question provides a more detailed response than the previous four research questions.

To determine the amount of time staff spent meeting funder compliance, we calculated the number of hours invested in each compliance task. (Compliance tasks were discussed in Chapter Two.) Directors and supervisors were asked how many hours on average per month were spent on each compliance activity. Figure 3.3 shows the mean number of hours for each task for directors and supervisors.[3]

---

[2]   One supervisor did not provide a response to this question.

[3]   Appendix D provides the distribution of time investment for each task for both directors and supervisors.

Figure 3.3
Management's Monthly Mean Number of Compliance Hours

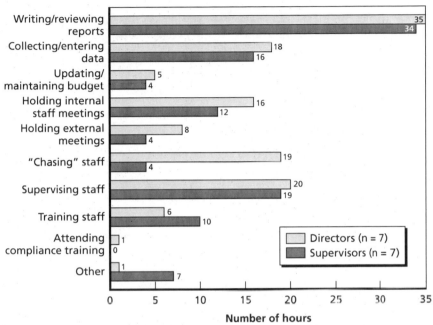

RAND *MG505-3.3*

As expected, the largest number of hours are spent writing and reviewing reports. Directors and supervisors spend approximately the same number of hours in an average month on this task. Again, given director and supervisor responsibilities, the next-substantial portion of time is dedicated to supervising staff (20 hours and 19 hours, respectively). The third highest time investment is data tracking and management, with directors spending an average of 18 hours per month and supervisors spending an average 16 hours per month. Directors spent the least amount of time, on average, attending compliance training sessions and other compliance activities. In contrast, supervisors spent an average of four hours per month on each of the following three activities: maintaining and tracking their budget, attending external meetings, and chasing staff for compliance-related information.

According to supervisors,[4] field staff spend as few as 32 hours to as many as 155 hours per month on compliance activities. On average, supervisors reported that field staff spent approximately 68 hours per month engaged in compliance activities, including writing reports, entering data, and tracking their budgets (shown on the left-hand side of Figure 3.4). The range is best explained by field staff duties. Field staff responsible for tracking incoming cases spend the vast majority of their time engaging in compliance-related activities, compared to treatment staff who divide their time between direct-service and compliance activities.

Results indicate that directors spend approximately 27 hours more on average per month on compliance activities than supervisors (see left-hand side of Figure 3.4). Directors' responsibilities may explain

Figure 3.4
Distribution of Total Mean Hours Spent on Compliance Activities by Staff Type

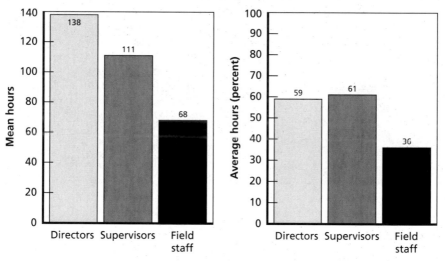

RAND MG505-3.4

---

[4] Focus group discussions addressed the types of activities field staff engage in and their experiences with those tasks. Given that direct supervisors track field staff work hours, they were asked about the number of hours field staff spend on compliance activities.

this difference. Directors are responsible for managing programs and responding to funder requests, as well as for synthesizing all summary reports provided by the supervisors who report to them. Supervisors reported spending an average of 43 hours more per month on compliance activities than their field staff. Given the number of reports produced by staff, it is not surprising to see this difference in time investment. Based on supervisor reports, staff spend approximately 68 hours a month on compliance tasks, which includes writing reports, tracking data, and maintaining budgets.

However, when comparing the percentage of time invested (the right-hand side of Figure 3.4), supervisors spend slightly more of their total hours on compliance tasks than do directors. This is because directors work slightly more hours per month on average (218 hours) compared to supervisors (214 hours). On average, field staff spend 36 percent of their time on compliance activities.

Total Hours Spent on Compliance Tasks

Table 3.4 provides a summary of total hours spent on compliance activities in the last fiscal year, showing that 44 percent of staff time was invested in compliance activities, such as writing reports, tracking data, and attending meetings, in the last fiscal year.

Table 3.4
Annual Compliance Hours for All Staff

Allocation of Hours	Hours (number and percent)
Total staff hours	97,822
Total compliance hours	42,794
Percentage of annual hours	44%

NOTE: These are totals for all staff interviewed for this study (n = 41).

Total Dollars Spent on Compliance Tasks

Figure 3.5 shows the average amount in wages spent on each compliance activity for management staff during the last fiscal year.[5] As expected, the largest average annual expenditure is on report writing and review by both directors and supervisors. The next-largest investment was in supervision. Attending compliance-related training received the least amount of annual funds.

Table 3.5 shows the total amount spent on salaries for all compliance activities. Based on the average number of hours invested in compliance and management salaries, this accounted for an average of

Figure 3.5
Mean Annual Dollars Spent on Management Staff, by Compliance Task

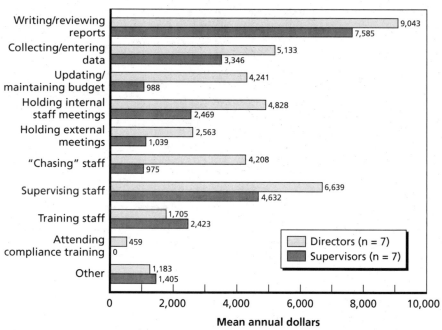

RAND MG505-3.5

---

[5] Appendix D provides a distribution of dollar investments by task type.

Table 3.5
Total Amount Spent on Compliance Activities

Allocation of Funding	Funding (amount and percent)
Total funding	$6,554,518
Total spent on compliance	$742,556
Percentage of total funding	11%

$742,556, which is approximately 11 percent of the annual budget.[6]

Given the lack of comparable studies, it is unclear whether 11 percent of an annual budget is significant or acceptable. Also, it is unclear whether 44 percent of staff time on funding compliance tasks is excessive. If we examine the challenges experienced by staff and the number of steps and staff involved in carrying out a compliance activity, such as a staff report, we can infer that time and dollars invested can be redirected to reduce undue burden, duplication, and delays.

Recommendations by Management and Field Staff

To address some of the challenges in meeting funder compliance, staff were asked for their recommendations at the agency and funder levels to improve performance and reduce time and dollar investments. Below is a summary of staff recommendations.

Agency-Level Recommendations by Staff. We derived six recommendations at this level. As with the previous sections, the categories reported below were derived from individual and focus group interviews. Therefore, results are reported by recommendation rather than staff type.

- *Provide a client information system and sufficient training.* PFF is in the process of installing an agency-wide data system for staff to use to create reports, update records, and share files with others.

---

[6] For the predefined funding sources.

Staff recommend that sufficient training be offered, as well as laptop computers and encrypted access to such computers, which will enable staff to access their files while off site. Staff suggested that this will reduce travel time and decrease the probability of becoming noncompliant.

- *Improve staff management.* Management and field staff said they feel demoralized by the way they are treated. One supervisor said, "Better support of middle management and other staff [is needed]," as is "recognition for [quality] performance." This reflects the sentiment expressed by field staff as well.
- *Improve internal compliance protocol.* Staff at all three levels said they would like to see an improvement in how compliance activities, such as reports, are carried out. To date, each program has its own protocol that may or may not work for staff. Unfortunately, the differences in protocol have created stressful situations for staff when information is needed from other programs for which the protocol is unknown or not established. Staff suggested that an agency-wide procedure for carrying out compliance activities would make expectations clear, reduce internal tensions, and increase productivity.
- *Educate staff about compliance issues and consequences.* Staff felt that education is needed about the importance of meeting compliance. However, given that meeting compliance is a means to ensuring the organization's vitality, this is a recommendation that would benefit the agency as a whole.
- *Provide parking.* This recommendation was voiced primarily by field staff, who may be required to write and file reports on site, which requires that they come to the office at varying times of the day. Given the limited number of parking spaces and the high cost of metered parking, this has created a barrier to completing reports on time.
- Other recommendations that were made included teaching better time management skills.

Funder Recommendations by Staff. With regard to funder rec-ommendations,[7] staff made five suggestions. Again, these recommen-dations are categories derived from the data.

- *Clarify requests.* Staff said that requests by funders are often unclear or vague. One supervisor said she would like to see funders "be much more specific regarding use of information and what [is] required." Having more specific information about the type of data or information necessary to fill the request is vital for meeting compliance.
- *Simplify requests.* Staff said they would like requests to be simplified.
- *Become aware of agency services and staff demands.* Staff suggested that funders and their respective staff members could become more aware of the type of services provided by the agency when making recommendations or requests. One staff member put it plainly, "[Funders need] more education of staff so they better understand [the] services [we provide] to families." Addition-ally, staff said funders should be aware of the number and type of demands placed on staff to ensure that funder requests are realistic.
- *Provide accurate and up-to-date information.* As one manager said, "Inaccurate information makes goal-setting difficult."
- Other recommendations included improving communication between funder staff and agency staff.

---

[7] These are recommendations made by staff. In some instances, some staff did not have any recommendations.

CHAPTER FOUR

Conclusions and Recommendations

In this section, we provide our conclusions, followed by some recommendations.

Conclusions

This study was guided by five research questions aimed at eliciting the challenges and costs associated with meeting funder compliance. Staff from a local nonprofit were asked about their staffing decisions, staffing challenges, training on compliance tasks, and time invested in the various relevant activities, and the amount spent in hours and dollars during last fiscal year was computed.

What we found is that staffing decisions are predetermined by a person's job description. Staffing challenges ranged from poor staff performance to overwhelmed staff. A closer examination of staff training showed that staff are not receiving adequate training in these tasks, which might explain why management staff reported field staff shortcomings as a staffing challenge. General challenges reported included all parties involved—funders, the agency, and internal staff—suggesting that no one entity or group is primarily responsible for challenges experienced by staff. However, these challenges varied across staff. Management staff felt that the lack of internal agency protocol is a key factor, while field staff saw funders as the primary barrier and put equal burden on the agency and internal staff.

Numerous data challenges were cited by staff interviewed for this study, including limited access to necessary data, inadequate internal data, poor data computation methods, tedious data requested by funders, and unreliable internal staff. The primary data challenge for management staff is access to the data, while field staff said that the quality of the data was their primary challenge.

With regard to staff's last compliance activities, five types of experiences were expressed, with the majority of directors and field staff reporting that the experience was stressful because of the type of data funders requested or because of the short turnaround time allowed to provide the necessary data. Supervisors said they experienced a mix of stress, resulting from the lack of internal agency protocol and from the routine nature of their last experience.

The cost of meeting funder compliance was presented in hours and dollars. On average, staff spent 44 percent of their time meeting funder compliance. This translates into 11 percent of agency funding. Pollak and Rooney (2003) found that nonprofits in their study reported spending anywhere from 0 to 100 percent of their budgets on management and general expenses, which indicates serious reporting problems. Gunz, Macnaughton, and Wensley (1995) found that companies in their study spent 1 to 3.4 percent of their grant funds on meeting funder compliance. However, some companies included time spent getting the grant and other related activities, making the actual costs of meeting funder compliance difficult to pin down. Our study found that 11 percent of the PFF's funds were spent on compliance activities. While 11 percent may be difficult to situate because of a lack of comparison data, this study is one of the most accurate accounts of an organization's compliance-related expenditures, making future comparisons possible.

Recommendations

The recommendations provided by staff in Chapter Three should be taken seriously. Staff members know best what is required to do their jobs and know the realities they face when meeting funder compliance. Fortunately, the challenges reported by staff can be resolved and the recommendations can be feasibly implemented. The primary issue is infrastructure: The organization lacks the necessary systems to ensure the lowest amount of staff investment for the highest level of performance. Therefore, we recommend that the organization spend some resources identifying individuals in the organization who can develop an internal compliance protocol that is consistent and realistic.

In addition, we recommend that field staff gain more training. It would benefit the entire organization if field staff received the appropriate amount of training to carry out the various compliance tasks, such as writing reports. In this same vein, field staff must possess basic skills, such as typing. When reports must be handwritten and typed by an assistant, additional dollars and time are wasted. Therefore, management should ensure that all staff have the necessary skills to carry out the important tasks necessary to maintain the vitality of the organization.

Finally, we recommend that the executive director identify an internal committee or external consulting firm to deal with the internal tensions among staff members. It was clear during the interviews and in the results collected that many staff members are not happy with the way the organization is being managed. In fact, several staff members said that the organization was at its best when the executive director had a hand in the daily management of the organization. Staff also said they have stayed with the organization because of the executive director, his mission, and the families they serve. Therefore, we highly recommend that the executive director either return to managing the staff on a more regular basis or teach other directors his practices so that he does not carry the sole responsibility of keeping the organization intact.

The recommendations provided here for the study site can be extended to the larger nonprofit community. Specifically, we recommend that executive directors or agency heads evaluate the organization's efficiency when meeting funder compliance while exploring barriers or challenges to carrying out those tasks. It is very likely that other organizations are experiencing similar staff challenges and related general challenges and are making time and money investments comparable to those of the study site. Therefore, it would be beneficial for all nonprofits to conduct an evaluation, at the individual and organization level, of the organization's policies and procedures for meeting funder compliance to determine if the existing protocol should be revised or replaced. For organizations in which duplication is occurring and staff members are investing a substantial amount of time on compliance tasks, excessive dollars are surely spent. This study provides an opportunity to examine those expenditures and find ways of saving money or reallocating funds to more profitable activities, such as fundraising and mission-related goals.

With regard to funders, we recommend that funders evaluate their data collection methods and types of requests to ensure that they collect pertinent data that will inform all participants (e.g., agency, funder, client, and staff), consider the burden placed on staff, consider how the data requested are being used, and explore an exchange related to compliance that is sensitive to the power differential between agency and funder.

Management Staff Interview Protocol

Forbes Funds: Case Study

Management Staff Interview Protocol

Date:_____
Start Time:_____
End Time:_____

Thank you for agreeing to meet with me. Just to reiterate, all of the information you share with me today will be kept confidential. I will assign an identification number that will be used to identify you. Pseudonyms (false names) will be used. Your real name will not be used or revealed. Do you have any questions so far?

The interview will take approximately 60 minutes. The purpose of the interview is to first learn about your experience and the kinds of things you do to help the organization meet funder compliance. The other purpose is to learn about your personal experience with regard to tasks associated with meeting compliance. Again, all of the information you share with me will be kept confidential.

Do you have any questions for me before we begin? Great! Let's get started.

Section A: Background

In this first section, I will ask you about your personal background, such as your age. I will ask you about your professional work experience.

1. Can you give me your initials?_____

2. What is the title of your position?_____

3. When did you begin to work for the organization?_____

4. Have you always had this position/job?
    No   0
    Yes   1 (Go to Q.5)

4a. What was the title of your previous position?_____

4b. How long did you hold that position?

4c. Did you have other positions (before the position in Q.4a)?
    No   0 (Go to Q.5)
    Yes   1

4d. Please tell me the title of those positions and the length of time you had each job:_____

_____

_____

5. How long have you had your current position?_____

6. What skills are necessary for your current position?_____

_____

_____

Section B: Compliance Tasks

Now, I would like to turn our attention to the types of tasks you're involved in with respect to meeting compliance. In thinking about these activities, I would like you to think about the amount of time you spend on each of these tasks. I'm going to ask you about the tasks for 4 different funding streams: County, State (e.g., VOCA), Foundation, and United Way. If you don't know which is which, we can talk in terms of programs.

1. Can you tell me the different types of tasks associated with meeting the following funder compliance tasks (e.g., writing reports, tracking data, etc.)?

Task	County	State	United Way	Foundation
a.				
b.				
c.				
d.				
e.				
f.				
g.				
h.				
i.				
j.				
k.				
l.				
m.				
n.				
o.				
p.				

2. Thinking back on the last fiscal year, how many hours on average do you spend *per month* on each of the following activities?

	Hours				
Task	County	State	United Way	Foundation	Total
a. Writing and reviewing reports					
b. Collecting and/or entering data (client information, outcomes, demographics, etc.)					
c. Updating and maintaining the budget					
d. Internal staff meetings regarding compliance tasks					
e. External staff meetings regarding compliance tasks					
f. "Chasing" staff for information/data					
g. Supervising staff					
h. Training staff					
i. Other:					
j. Other:					
k. Other:					
l. Other:					

3. How is the data tracked? (mark all that apply)

	County	State	United Way	Foundation(s)
a. Pencil and paper				
b. Computer program/software				
c. Email				
d. Phone or person-to-person conversation				
e. Other:				

4. I'd like you to think about all of the people, including yourself, involved in carrying out the various compliance tasks we've discussed today. Can you please provide the following information for all staff who participate, directly or indirectly, in those activities?

Initials	Education Level	Position/Title	Age	Gender	Race/Ethnicity	Number of Hours Scheduled to Work	Actual Number of Hours Worked	Hourly Rate/ Salary	Percent of Time Spent on Compliance Tasks
1.	1 2 3 4 5 6			1 2	1 2 3 4 5 6				
2.	1 2 3 4 5 6			1 2	1 2 3 4 5 6				
3.	1 2 3 4 5 6			1 2	1 2 3 4 5 6				
4.	1 2 3 4 5 6			1 2	1 2 3 4 5 6				
5.	1 2 3 4 5 6			1 2	1 2 3 4 5 6				
6.	1 2 3 4 5 6			1 2	1 2 3 4 5 6				
7.	1 2 3 4 5 6			1 2	1 2 3 4 5 6				
8.	1 2 3 4 5 6			1 2	1 2 3 4 5 6				
9.	1 2 3 4 5 6			1 2	1 2 3 4 5 6				
10.	1 2 3 4 5 6			1 2	1 2 3 4 5 6				
11.	1 2 3 4 5 6			1 2	1 2 3 4 5 6				

NOTES: Education Level: 1 = Less than high school; 2 = high school/general equivalency diploma; 3 = vocational; 4 = BS/BA; 5 = master's degree; 6 = Ph.D. Gender: 1 = female; 2 = male. Race/Ethnicity: 1 = white, non-Hispanic; 2 = African American/black, non-Hispanic; 3 = Hispanic/Latino; 4 = Asian/Pacific Islander; 5 = Native American; 6 = Other.

Section C: Staff and Compliance Tasks
Now I would like to ask you about staffing issues associated with compliance tasks.

1. Are you responsible for delegating compliance tasks to other staff?
   No   0 (Go to Q.3)
   Yes   1

2. How do you make staffing decisions? (Circle all that apply.)

   1.   Job description
   1.   Ability
   2.   Training/skills
   3.   Availability
   4.   Prior experience
   5.   Office protocol
   6.   Funder expertise
   7.   Other:
   8.   Other:
   9.   Other:

3. Not including staff we have already discussed, are other staff involved in tracking the data, such as an administrative assistant?
   No   0 (Go to Q.4)
   Yes   1

3a. Can you provide the following information for each of those individuals?

Initials	Education Level	Position/Title	Age	Gender	Race/Ethnicity	Number of Hours Scheduled to Work	Actual Number of Hours Worked	Hourly Rate/ Salary	Percent of Time Spent on Compliance Tasks
1.	1 2 3 4 5 6			1 2	1 2 3 4 5 6				
2.	1 2 3 4 5 6			1 2	1 2 3 4 5 6				
3.	1 2 3 4 5 6			1 2	1 2 3 4 5 6				
4.	1 2 3 4 5 6			1 2	1 2 3 4 5 6				
5.	1 2 3 4 5 6			1 2	1 2 3 4 5 6				
6.	1 2 3 4 5 6			1 2	1 2 3 4 5 6				
7.	1 2 3 4 5 6			1 2	1 2 3 4 5 6				
8.	1 2 3 4 5 6			1 2	1 2 3 4 5 6				
9.	1 2 3 4 5 6			1 2	1 2 3 4 5 6				
10.	1 2 3 4 5 6			1 2	1 2 3 4 5 6				
11.	1 2 3 4 5 6			1 2	1 2 3 4 5 6				

NOTES: Education Level: 1 = Less than high school; 2 = high school/general equivalency diploma; 3 = vocational; 4 = BS/BA; 5 = master's degree; 6 = Ph.D. Gender: 1 = female; 2 = male. Race/Ethnicity: 1 = white, non-Hispanic; 2 = African American/black, non-Hispanic; 3 = Hispanic/Latino; 4 = Asian/Pacific Islander; 5 = Native American; 6 = Other.

4. What are the staffing challenges in meeting funder compliance? For example, is there a disconnect between available staff and staff capable of engaging in compliance-related tasks?_____

_____

_____

_____

_____

Section D: Subjective Experience

In this final section, I would like to ask about your experience in meeting compliance tasks.

1. Thinking back on your most recent reports/compliance activities, how would you describe those experiences?_____

_____

_____

_____

_____

2. Thinking back on those past reports/compliance activities, what would you do differently?__ _____

_____

_____

_____

_____

3. What is most challenging in carrying out compliance-related tasks? (Provide examples.)_____

_____

_____

_____

_____

4. What are the data challenges in meeting compliance?_____

_____

_____

_____

_____

5. What changes would you make at an agency level?_____

_____

_____

6. Would you like to make any recommendation to funders related to compliance tasks?_____

_____

_____

_____

7. Do you feel that all your skills are being used?_____

_____

_____

_____

8. What additional skills do you think you need?_____

_____

_____

_____

9. What is the most rewarding aspect of meeting funder compliance?

_____

_____

_____

_____

10. Is there anything else you would like to add?_____

_____

_____

_____

_____

Well, those are all of my questions. Do you have any questions for me? May I contact you with any follow-up questions?

Field Staff Interview Focus Group Protocol

Forbes Funds: Case Study

Field Staff Focus Group Interview Protocol

Date:_____
Start Time:_____
End Time:_____

Thank you for agreeing to meet with me. Just to reiterate, all of the information you share with me today will be kept confidential. I will assign an identification number that will be used to identify you. Pseudonyms (false names) will be used. Your real name will not be used or revealed. Do you have any questions so far?

The interview will take approximately 45 minutes. The purpose of the interview is to first learn about your experience and the kinds of things you do to help the organization meet funder compliance. The other purpose is to learn about your personal experience with regard to tasks associated with meeting compliance. Again, all of the information you share with me will be kept confidential.

Before we begin the discussion, I would like to ask you to fill out a short survey. Please fold your survey and place it in the attached envelope.

[*Hand surveys to participants.*]

Please feel free to let me know if you have any questions. Again, all of the information will be kept confidential. Numbers will be reported in averages. No one's personal information will be divulged.

[*Collect surveys.*]

Do you have any questions for me before we begin? Great! Let's get started.

Section A: Compliance Tasks

As some of you may know, I have been interviewing management regarding compliance tasks they are required to carry out for each program funder. In addition to speaking with them, I would like to learn more about the type of compliance activities you're engaged in and what that experience has been like for you. In particular, I would like you to think about your experience in the last fiscal year as well as this year. Your fiscal year runs from summer to summer.

1. I want to get a picture of the types of things you do to help the organization meet funder compliance. Can you tell me, with a show of hands, how many of you are involved in the following activities:

Task	Yes	No	Don't Know
a. Writing and reviewing reports			
b. Collecting and/or entering data (client information, outcomes, demographics, etc.)			
c. Updating and maintaining budgets			
d. Internal staff meetings regarding compliance tasks			
e. External staff meetings regarding compliance tasks			
f. "Chasing" staff for information/data			
g. Supervising staff			
h. Training staff			
i. Other:			
j. Other:			
k. Other:			
l. Other:			

2. For those of you who are writing reports and tracking data, how are the reports and data kept? (Mark all that apply.)

	Yes	No	Don't Know
a. Pencil and paper			
b. Computer program/software			
c. Email			
d. Phone or person-to-person conversation			
e. Other:			

3. Now I would like to learn more about the training you might have received in preparation for the reports and data tracking you're responsible for. Again, with a show of hands, how many of you have been formally trained, by your supervisor or another agency employee to:

Task	Yes	No	Don't Know
a. Write reports			
b. Collect and/or enter data (client information, outcomes, demographics, etc.)			
c. Update and maintain budgets			
d. Other:			
e. Other:			

Section B: Subjective Experience
In this final section, I would like to ask about your experience in carrying out these compliance tasks.

1. Thinking back on your most recent reports/data tracking, how would you describe those experiences?_____

_____

_____

_____

_____

2. Thinking back on those past reports/compliance activities, what would you do differently?_____

_____

_____

_____

_____

3. What is most challenging in carrying out compliance-related tasks? (Provide examples.)_____

_____

_____

_____

_____

4. What changes would you make at the agency level?_____

_____

_____

_____

_____

5. Would you like to make any recommendation to funders related to compliance tasks?_____

_____

_____

_____

_____

6. Do you feel that all your skills are being used?_____

_____

_____

_____

_____

7. What additional skills do you think you need?_____

_____

_____

_____

_____

8. What is the most rewarding aspect of meeting funder compliance?

_____

_____

_____

_____

_____

9. Is there anything else you would like to add?_____

_____

_____

_____

_____

Well, those are all of my questions. Do you have any questions for me? May I contact you with any follow-up questions?

Field Staff Confidential Interview Protocol

Forbes Funds: Case Study

Field Staff Confidential Interview Protocol: Confidential Survey

Date:_____
Start Time:_____
End Time:_____

 The interview will take approximately 45 minutes. The purpose of the interview is to first learn about your experience and the kinds of things you do to help the organization meet funder compliance. The other purpose is to learn about your personal experience with regard to tasks associated with meeting compliance. Again, all of the information you share with me will be kept confidential.

 Before we begin the discussion, I would like to ask you to fill out this short survey. Please fold your survey and place it in the attached envelope.

Personal Background
In this first section, I will ask you about your personal background, such as your age. I will ask you about your professional work experience.

1. Initials: _____

2. What is the title of your position?_____

3. When did you begin to work for the organization?_____

4. Have you always had this position/job?
 (Please Circle One)
 No 0
 Yes 1 (Go to Q.5)

 4a. What was the title of your previous position?_____

 4b. How long did you hold that position?_____

4c. Did you have other positions (prior to the position in Q.4a)?
(Please Circle One)
No   0 (Go to Q.5)
Yes   1

5. How long have you had your current position? _____

6. What skills are necessary for your current position?_____
_____
_____

7. What is your highest level of education? _____

8. What is your age?_____

9. Gender
(Please Circle One)
Female   1
Male   2

10. What is your race/ethnicity?
(Please Circle One)
White non-Hispanic   1
Hispanic   2
Black non-Hispanic   3
Asian/Pacific Islander   4
Other (   )   5

11. How are you paid?
(Please Circle One)
Hourly   1
Salary   2

12. How much are you paid (hourly/salary)?_____

13. Hours required to work per week:_____

14. Actual hours worked per week: _____

15. Days of the week required to work per week:_____

_____

Distribution of Compliance Hours

Table D.1
Director Compliance Hours

	n	Minimum	Maximum	Mean	Standard Deviation
Reports	7	0	86	35	35
Data	7	0	108	18	40
Budgets	7	0	38	10	16
Internal meetings	7	0	40	16	13
External meetings	7	0	23	8	8
Chasing staff	7	0	108	19	40
Supervision	7	0	101	21	36
Staff training	7	0	23	6	8
Attending training	7	0	10	1	4
Other	7	0	16	2	6

Table D.2
Supervisor Compliance Hours

	n	Minimum	Maximum	Mean	Standard Deviation
Reports	7	3	57	34	20
Data	7	4	60	16	20
Budgets	7	0	16	4	6
Internal meetings	7	0	36	12	13
External meetings	7	0	16	4	6
Chasing staff	7	0	20	4	7
Supervision	7	0	60	19	23
Staff training	7	0	34	10	12
Attending training	7	0	0	0	0
Other	7	0	26	7	11

Distribution of Compliance Dollars

Table E.1
Compliance Dollars for Directors

	N	Minimum ($)	Maximum ($)	Mean ($)	Standard Deviation ($)
Writing/reviewing reports	7	0	19,200	9,043	8,309
Collecting/entering data	7	0	26,500	5,133	9,897
Updating/ maintaining budgets	7	0	18,779	4,241	7,106
Holding internal meetings	7	0	11,501	4,828	3,981
Holding external meetings	7	0	7,228	2,563	2,555
"Chasing" staff	7	0	24,000	4,208	8,860
Supervising staff	7	0	31,321	6,639	11,080
Training staff	7	0	7,228	1,705	2,572
Attending training	7	0	3,212	459	1,214
Other	7	0	8,279	1,183	3,129

Table E.2
Compliance Dollars for Supervisors

	n	Minimum ($)	Maximum ($)	Mean ($)	Standard Deviation ($)
Writing/reviewing reports	7	436	13,865	7,585	4,771
Collecting/entering data	7	581	13,605	3,456	4,539
Updating/ maintaining budgets	7	0	3,628	988	1,366
Holding internal meetings	7	0	6,393	2,469	2,602
Holding external meetings	7	0	3,628	1,039	1,471
"Chasing" staff	7	0	4,858	975	1,781
Supervising staff	7	0	14,595	4,632	5,516
Training staff	7	0	8,565	2,423	3,121
Attending compliance training	7	0	0	0	0
Other	7	0	5,023	1,405	2,066

Bibliography

Charity Navigator, "Mid-Atlantic: Pennsylvania," undated. Online at http://www.charitynavigator.org/index.cfm?bay=search.cat&stid=31&rgid=2&sortby=name&FromRec=26 (as of April 10, 2006).

Gawande, Kishore, and Timothy Wheeler, "Measures of Effectiveness for Governmental Organizations," *Management Science*, Vol. 45, No. 1, January 1999, pp. 42–58.

Gammal, Denise L., Caroline Simard, Hokyu Hwang, and Walter W. Powell, *Managing Through Challenges: A Profile of San Francisco Bay Area Nonprofits*, Stanford, Calif.: Stanford Project on the Evolution of Nonprofits, Center for Social Innovation, Stanford Graduate School of Business, 2005. Online at http://www.gsb.stanford.edu/csi/pdf/SPEN_Stanford_Study_on_the_Evolution_of_Nonprofits.pdf (as of March 28, 2006).

Glazer, Barney G., and Anselm L. Strauss, *The Discovery of Grounded Theory: Strategies for Qualitative Research*, Chicago, Ill.: Aldine, 1967.

Gunz, Sally, Alan Macnaughton, and Karen Wensley, "Measuring the Compliance Costs of Tax Expenditures: The Case of Research and Development Incentives, *Canadian Tax Journal*, Vol. 43, No. 6, 1995, pp. 2008–2034.

Hager, Mark, and Janet Greenlee, "How Important Is a Nonprofit's Bottom Line? The Uses and Abuses of Financial Data," in Peter Frumkin and Jonathan B. Imber, eds., *In Search of the Nonprofit Sector*, New Brunswick, N.J.: Transaction Publishers, 2004, pp. 85–96.

Helburn, Suzanne W., et al., *Cost, Quality, and Child Outcomes in Child Care Centers*, Vols. 1 and 2, Technical Report, National Center for Early Development and Learning, Denver, Colo.: University of Colorado at Denver, Department of Economics, Center on Research and Social Policy, 1995.

Karoly, Lynn A., M. Rebecca Kilburn, James H. Bigelow, Jonathan P. Caulkins, and Jill S. Cannon, *Assessing Costs and Benefits of Early Childhood Intervention Programs: Overview and Application to the Starting Early, Starting Smart Program*, Santa Monica, Calif.: RAND Corporation, MR-1336-CFP, 2001. Online at http://www.rand.org/pubs/monograph_reports/MR1336/ (as of March 29, 2006).

Keim, Kathryn S., Marilyn A. Swanson, Sandra E. Cann, and Altragracia Salinas, "Focus Group Methodology: Adapting the Process for Low-Income Adults and Children of Hispanic and Caucasian Ethnicity," *Family and Consumer Sciences Research Journal*, Vol. 27, No. 4, 1999, pp. 451–465.

Pollak, Thomas H., and Patrick Rooney, "Management and General Expenses: The Other Half of Overhead," *The Nonprofit Quarterly*, Vol. 10, No. 1, Spring 2003, pp. 30–32.

Pollak, Thomas H., Patrick Rooney, and Mark A. Hager, "Understanding Management and General Expenses in Nonprofits," presented at the 2001 Annual Meeting of the Association for Research on Nonprofit Organizations and Voluntary Action, New Orleans, La., 2001. Online at http://nccsdataweb.urban.org/kbfiles/525/M&G.pdf (as of March 29, 2006).

Strauss, Anselm L., and Juliet Corbin, *Basics in Qualitative Research: Grounded Theory Procedures and Techniques*, Newbury Park, Calif.: Sage Publications, 1990.

Wing, Kennard, and Mark A. Hager, "The Quality of Financial Reporting by Nonprofits: Findings and Implications," Policy Brief, Nonprofit Overhead Cost Project, Urban Institute Center on Philanthropy, Indiana University, Bloomington, Ind., August 1, 2004. Online at http://www.urban.org/url.cfm?ID=311045 (as of March 29, 2006).